ALSO BY JOHN KOETHE

THE SWIMMER

Farrar, Straus and Giroux

NEW YORK

The
Swimmer

John
Koethe

Farrar, Straus and Giroux
18 West 18th Street, New York 10011

Printed in the United States of America
First edition, 2016

Library of Congress Cataloging-in-Publication Data
Koethe, John, 1945–
   [Poems. Selections]
   The swimmer / John Koethe. — First edition.
      pages ; cm
   ISBN 978-0-374-27232-6 (hardcover) —
   ISBN 978-0-374-71377-5 (e-book)
   I. Title.

PS3561.O35A6 2016
811'.54—dc23

                           2015022231

Designed by Quemadura

www.fsgbooks.com
www.twitter.com/fsgbooks
www.facebook.com/fsgbooks

10 9 8 7 6 5 4 3 2 1

TO MARK STRAND

CONTENTS

I

I

THE ARROGANCE OF PHYSICS

The twentieth century was the century of physics:
The physical world came close to being tamed
By understanding, making it harder to understand
Or even imagine, on the scale of the cosmos
And on the order of the very small: time passes
As your twin ages, while you remain perpetually young—
Though a lot of good it does you, existing as you do
At no place in particular, smeared out everywhere
Until someone sees you and your wave packet collapses.

It was also the century of poetry, modern poetry
And the question it engendered, which it keeps repeating:
"Are you just going to go on writing poems like this,
Writing for posterity? Posterity isn't interested
Unless you are, because instead of a quaint immortality,
It offers merely intermittent moments of attention
Before moving on, maybe to return, but probably not.
You can't displace your heroes in the pantheon,
Because there isn't one: just this giant, happy band
Of suppliants, each one knowing what the others know.
I realize this isn't what you'd hoped for, but please,
Don't get discouraged—celebrate temporality instead."

∎

So here I am, sitting in a park thirty years after writing
"In the Park," a poem I'd hoped might last forever.
They finally discovered the Higgs boson, which means that
Physics is still on track, though no one knows to where.
I still believe in it, of course, though it's so removed
From everything I think I think there's nothing to imagine
Beyond equations, which is fine — it was equations all the way,
Until I came to poetry and knew that it was what I had to do.
And now look where I am, what I've become: a marginal observer
Of a universe of my own devising, waiting on a dénouement that
    never comes,
But that continues through an afternoon that's wider than the sky,
    whose
Mild, unearthly blue conceals an emptiness resounding like a
    gong
Tolling for no one, while I sit here in the safety of my song. Like
    the hedgehog,
I still know what I know, although it matters not at all: I labor
    over it,
And yet it's written in a different idiom, full of sound and fury,
Signifying — what? It can't be nothing, though it might as well be
If it can't be rendered in the language of the stars. I want to
Speak to something far away, beyond the confines of the page,
But it won't listen, and to everything I say it answers No.

THE LONG DISSOLVE

Go, get you home, you fragments! CORIOLANUS

You start at home, and most of your life
Elaborates a first idea of home: a place you've
Been and think you'll always be, a place
You know you can return to, full of comforting
Presences like rural or domestic buildings,
So abstract it isn't even real. I began there,
And now it all seems strange to me:
The stories that it tells, the stories I told,
Seem discontinuous and small, as though they're
No one's stories anymore, those of an author
Who'd lost interest in them, and was old. A sudden
Breeze sweeps through the vacant lots, scattering leaves
And cellophane, the miscellaneous detritus of a life.
Like scraps of paper carried by the breeze from home
To here, and then a figure walking towards me
Across an open field, coming from the vast distance
Things tend towards, they come at last to me: the quick,
Unmediated thoughts, secure in their final home,
That have their say and stand apart and make no sense.
I've spent my life like this. I'm sick of it, and tired.
Why can't I say what I mean? I saw a movie
That felt this way: an open field, a breeze that blew

From nowhere, trash collecting on a fence. It was
Another person's, though I took it for my own:
The scenes that had immured me silently dissolved
As the credits unrolled, leaving an almost empty screen
And a highway leading somewhere off the page.
I tried to picture anywhere but here, a place
Beyond the indifference and infirmities of age,
But there was nothing, nothing I could see.
I felt elated for a moment, and complete.
But then I knew it was where I had to go.

FRANK SINATRA'S TRAINS

Let's fly away!

Who knew? All Ol' Blue Eyes signified to me
Was *Sinatra at the Sands*, *Come Fly with Me*,
Dean Martin, Sammy Davis Jr. and the Rat Pack
And Pvt. Angelo Maggio dying in *From Here to Eternity*.
My tax guy came this week. His hobby is collecting
Model trains, and since he does my girlfriend's taxes too
I mentioned her new job at Kalmbach Publishing,
Publisher of *Model Railroader* (as of course he knew).
He'd just bought some of Johnny Carson's trains
In an online auction, and told me Neil Young
And someone I can't remember were collectors too,
And that the Holy Grail of model train collecting
(It blew me away) was Frank Sinatra's Lionel trains,
Whose whereabouts since his death no one knew.

It resonates with me. Model trains and music
Were my (part-time) hobbies too: I loved that minor
League Sinatra, Bobby Darin, and I still do,
And even though my trains all vanished long ago,
Like those "thrilling returning trains" of Nick Carraway's
Youth or Frank Sinatra's, sometimes the acrid
Smell of artificial smoke drifts back to me

Across the years—my Rosebud or my madeleine—
And I'm twelve again, here in the warm September of my years.
It's funny how we go from nowhere in particular to home,
And from a past implicit in the present to the minor
Dispensations of these hours, or from eternity to here—
Waiting for an accountant, browsing through some
Magazines about toy trains or stereos, while all the while
The adolescent possibilities are lingering somewhere
In the dark, biding their time, waiting to be inhabited again.

Up the lazy river, where the songs keep rolling past
And where the trains come 'round the plaster mountains
Down in the basement, on the road to Mandalay.
Sometimes I strain to hear the music through the traffic,
But it's always there, like death and taxes.
Why can't life be a hobby, filled with jokes and poems,
And poems like jokes, instead of the encounter
With eternity we make it out to be? I like to think of
Li'l Blue Eyes in the basement, working the controls
While in the background you can hear the lyrics of "Brazil,"
With friends and Cokes and chips and someone's father
Looking proudly on at what he'd made. I like to make things up,
As though remembering at last some long-ago cacophony
Of clangs and whistles and the distant smell of artificial smoke.

VON FREEMAN

I was a rock-and-roll child. I saw Elvis
Truncated by Ed Sullivan, listened to Fats Domino
Sing "Blueberry Hill" and loved "Sixteen Tons,"
Which was proto–rock and roll. I still love it,
But since you can't remain a child forever,
I cast my net wider, and thanks to my Japanese
Integrated amp, saxophones wash over me each night.
It started with Paul Desmond, who aspired to sound
"Like a dry martini," and went on to bring to life
The celebrated and obscure alike: Spike Robinson,
Whom I heard at the Jazz Estate a few blocks away
In 1992; Frank Morgan, who had Milwaukee ties
And whom I wanted to nominate for an honorary degree,
A scam set up for local businessmen; and Coltrane
Of course, that endless aural rope that curls upon itself
And then uncoils. And it wasn't simply saxophones: Chet
Baker's trumpet, plangent and permanent as he fell from
Young and beautiful to wrecked and toothless; and Bill Evans,
Still perfecting "Autumn Leaves" at Top of the Gate,
While downstairs in the streets the '60s boiled. Von Freeman
Died last week at 88. I hadn't heard of him until he died,
And now here he is, filling up my room with "Time After Time."
He believed in roughness, and on leaving imperfections in

So his songs wouldn't lose their souls, which is how I think of poems.
Philip Larkin loved jazz too—a great poet, though disagreeable—
But I don't know if other poets on my radar do. Maybe they
Think it's easy, I say to myself as I put on a record of Mal Waldron's,
To whom Billie Holiday once whispered a song along a keyboard
In the 5 Spot and Frank O'Hara and everyone stopped breathing.

MISS HEATON

She was probably younger than I remember her—
A small, white-haired lady who taught Honors English
To twelfth-graders. I was sixteen, completely gone
On math and physics, though I had an "amateur" interest
In modern literature, the more advanced the better,
Which was probably due to mathematics: Faulkner, Joyce,
Virginia Woolf, wherever the stream of consciousness meandered.
She disapproved: "Why don't you read some Thomas Hardy?"
She suggested while I was working on an Advanced Placement
Essay on "Daffodils" or "Stopping by Woods on a Snowy Evening"
(I don't remember which). Eight years ago someone who
Likes my poetry emailed "Proud Songsters," a poem about some
    birds—
Thrushes, finches, nightingales—who before they assumed the
    form of song
And feathers were just "particles of grain, / And earth, and air,
    and rain."
I liked the nihilism and the lyricism, then forgot about it,
As I usually do with poems. This week that poem came back
    to me,
A breath of genius on a tiny, human scale, by contrast with the
Strenuous heroics of high modernism and the mathematical
    sublime

That have now become a visionary ideal no one aspires to anymore,
Because it can't—it can't what? I'm a sucker for the subtle
     sentimental,
And I even like it, though I disapprove. I wouldn't say Miss Heaton
Won, and yet I'm moved, without wanting to be moved and against
     my better
Judgment. Of course the way I write is different (so I like to think),
But a pernicious continuity keeps creeping in. Still, I want to
Keep that tiny flame alive, to keep insisting on the difference,
     even if
The difference may be no more than insouciance with a slight
Heightening at the end, as if Thomas Hardy were sipping a martini.

THE JAPANESE AESTHETIC

Precise and rough at the same time, physical and clear,
It engages me the way my father's bonsais never did, too
Artful and contrived. "It looks like a lump of mud,"
Diane said of my latest acquisition, an anagama
Excrescence of clay, a vaguely lidded vessel form
Sitting on the bookcase amid the pots by other potters—
Toshiko Takaezu, Shio Kusaka, Laura Andreson
(Who wasn't Japanese, though the aesthetic holds)—
Across the living room from the Leben ("A Motion Sound")
Tubed stereo components that recall the '50s in their nostalgia
For the natural. There's such pleasure sitting here, looking
And listening at the same time: materiality is the point,
Texture, coarseness, stuff—call it what you will.
You put some clay or words into the furnace and wait
For what emerges from the fire once it's died down.

Why do I go on writing lyrics of the small occasions
Whose symbolism is so obvious? The Japanese aesthetic
Is literal and unembellished, utilitarian and crude
And beautiful. No one believes in beauty anymore,
Except by default, and yet it's everywhere: in the imperfections
In the clay, the exaggerated tenor of the tenor saxophone
Playing "Time After Time" while time slips away, in all the little
Accidents that make the days go by. You'd think it can't be planned,

But leave it there, alone, and see what happens. I'm constantly
Surprised by what I didn't know I knew, by what I find by
     inattention—
Though the danger is to let that random beauty carry you away
Until the clay and cat shit and the words vanish into pure
Perception, with nothing there to see. They make cars too.

SARTOR RESARTUS

What is it with men's clothes? It isn't about
How you look or even who or what you are,
But about twin fantasies of appearance and identity:
The way you see yourself, the way you'd like to seem
In the eyes of a beholder, in a daydream, in reality.
My high school friend Tom Agsten was addicted too:
The perfect khaki pants, the madras shirts, cordovan Florsheim
Shoes. "Why do you like dressing well?" he asked,
And when I said I didn't know, he told me why he did:
"It's because it makes me feel I'm better than other people."

Don't think Leopold and Loeb. There was always something
More important (*this*, for instance), but it was always there.
I studied it in college, where I learned that making clothes seem
Unimportant was the point—the frayed Brooks Brothers collar
Or the white Brooks Brothers button-down you wore with a tuxedo
To a deb party, parties where you hung around till dawn.
Style was the point—a style of seeming unconcerned with style
To the point of an obsession, though the stores all stayed the same:
Brooks, J. Press, Paul Stuart, stores long gone now to their graves
Like Chipp and Langrock, F. R. Tripler, Sulka, stores that lined
    Fifth Avenue
When it was lined with gold. The sixties might have ruined things,
But then that way of life became a look, a theoretical conceit,

A whole philosophy of clothes that you could read about
On askandyaboutclothes.com. You could study it anywhere,
Which made it meaningless, as meaningless as fashion.

It all seems quaint—the khakis, madras shirts and Florsheim shoes
(Jack Nicholson in *Chinatown*: "Goddamn Florsheim shoe!")—
And yet I still inhabit that obsession, now divorced from
All connection with reality or sense of purpose: Caraceni
And Bardelli jackets, brown suede shoes, an Arnys Forestière,
All hanging in my closet waiting for their day. Two weeks ago
I bought another navy blazer—that makes five or six,
Depending on how you count them—that I didn't need.
The days go by online, or like pages of a catalog turning
In my mind from suits to coats to shirts to ties to shoes.
There's nothing much to do but watch the interplay of memory
And fancy as they flow across a page, or animate my own
Community of two or three residing in my head.
Sometimes I think of poetry the way I think of clothes:
A feigned indifference disguising a compulsion
With no purpose but its own. My friends are all here,
All on the same page, if only momentarily,
Until the spell breaks like the emperor's new clothes
That can't conceal the fact there's no one there,
Though I hate that easy irony. Anyway,
We're all dressed up. Now, where shall we go?

SKINNY POEM

write some skinny poems

JAMES SCHUYLER

Life is rough, as
Rough as you make it.
Is it better to be the
Best at something, or is a
Gentleman's C enough,
At least occasionally?
I used to think it was—
I used to think whatever
Felt like thought was sheer
Pleasure, but I'm old now:
It's all edges, edges and
Scraps, like a collage.
I thought that continuity
Was everything, and now I
Think it's a mirage, like a
Sound effect or an echo,
A reflection of what flows
Inexorably beneath. "Man
Is the measure of all things":
Protagoras. Plato refuted
Him, to no avail—you can't

Argue with a blank stare:
"Here I stand." I hate poems
Of affirmation, poems too
Unaware, too smooth
To be true. Life is rough.

LITTLE GUYS WHO LIVE HERE

Speaking of cats, when was the last
time you spoke to one, calling it by its name?
JOHN ASHBERY

I sing the cat. Or rather, I sing the small
Animals we keep in our houses, of which cats
Are the prime example. Edgar Allan Poe's
Black Cat notwithstanding—that thing with the hot
Breath and burning eyes—they make you feel at home
In your house, which might otherwise feel empty.
I like to wake up to a cat—a white one in my case—
That's helped me make it through the night
By sleeping on a pad (the "Mysterious Purr Padd")
At the foot of my bed, with forays to my side
To "cuddle," if that's the word, and a nose
Like a cold blossom. I used to have two cats:
The eponymous Chester of another poem of mine,
And Douglas, who made Chester miserable.

They loom larger in their absence than their presence,
Once you've become accustomed to their faces.
There isn't much to do but stare at them
And scratch their ears and wait for their kidneys to fail.
Cat mortality may not seem like the stuff of tragedy,

Yet losing something that's become a part of you,
However small, isn't easy, as Diane discovered
After coming home from the vet's for the last time
To "the silence after the viaticum" and an empty house—
Though in my case Douglas was still there, bothered
By the empty carrying case, and a changed cat thereafter.
Of course we project ourselves onto them, just as we
Project ourselves onto each other, but with this difference:
We have "souls," whatever that might mean, while cats are cute,
And in a way "cute" is all they are. "Such a good guy,"
I keep muttering as he snuggles up at 4 a.m., until I no longer
Know what I mean, and it grows cold from repetition.

"I am Lord of all I survey," I think to myself,
Sitting on the deck of my house in the country, before
Coming home to find I haven't been missed at all:
Douglas sitting on his pad, his small, gruff face
Hiding a deep indifference deflating any pretensions
To transcendence or grandiosity, disdainful as the
Dowagers in one of my favorite *New Yorker* cartoons
Emerging from a performance of *Murder in the Cathedral*:
"Such a disappointment. And from the author of *Cats*!"

A COUPLA YEGGS

I always thought yeggs were something like schmucks,
Although they're really safecrackers, though no one knows why.
According to Wikipedia, "schmuck" meant penis in Yiddish,
But because of its vulgarity it got euphemized to "schmo,"
Which became the basis for the vile Al Capp's Schmoos
(The precursors, if you ask me, of Smurfs). "A coupla yeggs"—
I probably read it in a Damon Runyon story, who was my favorite
Writer for a while after college, after Proust. "Get the money"
Was Runyon's favorite saying according to Ted Berrigan,
Whom I didn't know well, but enjoyed seeing now and then.
John Godfrey and I would go into New York, wander around
And appropriate anything we could—a heady time for
Poetry, not just in New York but everywhere, when people
Argued about it and it mattered. There are no secrets anymore,
And everyone likes everything, which is even worse, but back then
Secrets were there for the taking, if you could crack their codes.
What made them so important? Call this poem Exhibit A
And forget "back then": what makes it important is the elation
Of being lost on the way to nowhere, walking with John or Diane or
Anyone through the big city like eternal out-of-towners, dazed
By its promise and hell-bent to crack its secrets, like a coupla yeggs.

MELANCHOLY OF THE AUTUMN GARDEN

IN MEMORIAM ROBERT DASH

The driveway to the winter house looks like that
Driveway in *Dead of Night* that leads back to a past
It started out from. I started going out there
In 1974, pre-Jitney: I'd take the train, and usually
I'd run into fellow travelers: Marjorie, or Bill and Willy,
Everyone went out there then. We'd linger around the table
Gesturing at reading the *Times*, planning long walks
And looking forward to the cocktail hour(s).
Darragh was always there, the window frames were white,
The garden was subdued, then it exploded into color,
Purples and pastels around the windows. "You've ruined it,"
Said Peter Schjeldahl, and that was it for him. Aladar
Came out in zippers and black leather: "Aladar,
You look just like a purse!" It was the funniest thing
I'd ever heard, which shows you just how giddy
The whole thing was, and why it couldn't last: drunken
Tedium amidst a beauty fashioned from the mind
As much as from the hand and dirt, and the beauty remains.
In time the others drifted one by one away, leaving me
To keep the flame alive, a solitary remnant.
The garden remains outwardly unchanged while changing

With the seasons and the years, beginning with the gentle greens
Of spring, then summer's colors, then warm
Autumn tones, until in mid-November it becomes inert.

"And we were drunk for month on month"
(Pound, *Cathay*), and look at where it leads: dialysis
Interminable, that's so excruciating one can faint.
We talked about Mabel Mercer: "All in all /
It was worth it." Was it really? Yes, of course it was,
But what the songs all try to say defies analysis:
There's no such thing as the completely wasted life,
Just lives of varying degrees of opacity and transparency,
Through which the limits of the visible appear.
Instead of years, their real measure is the underlying
Rationale, so hard to articulate, that no one understands,
Though it shows through. I remember walking through the garden
Without any clue beyond its beauty. There was something
Marjorie wanted me to say, and now I can't remember what it
    was—
Maybe something about gardens over time, who knows?
In spring it's open to the public, but now the view is mine alone,
Taking in the trees with no leaves left, the enclosure with its
    stubble,
Swaths of gray on gray, the simple placard reading Closed.
It's there for all to see, and yet its meaning lies beneath it or
    beyond it,

In the fantasies of its creator, which is to say, nowhere at all.
I digress, I acquiesce, I conjure what I want to see from nothing—
That's the way art works. It sounds like fantasies fulfilled,
And yet it's more a record of the things discarded on the way
To a mild November morning, watching the skull beneath the
   skin,
Or better still, a carapace from which the mortal flesh is gone.
The beauty is what's left. It doesn't make any sense, but there it is.

THE UNINVOLVED NARRATOR

His voice lost itself in the calm of the evening.

HEART OF DARKNESS

I'm witness to my life, but as for
Participating in it, I'll take the Fifth.
I wake up wondering what to do,
And as the day proceeds the answer
Keeps receding, until it's time for a drink
And dinner, music or a movie, and bed.
Sometimes I read, sometimes I just imagine
Being read about, like someone in a story.
Marlow said that Kurtz was ultimately a voice
"From the heart of an impenetrable darkness"
Repeating something to itself, exalted or contemptible,
"The pulsating stream of light, or the deceitful flow."
Gatsby, two decades hence (though it seems a century),
Was another one impossible to know but for the
Sheer perfection of the sentences surrounding him,
Spoken by someone standing to one side.
I'm not like them—I live and breathe, I have an
Inner life, but from your perspective all I am
Is another solitary voice, another would-be poet
Talking to himself about things of mutual concern
To who knows whom. Time is all we have in common,

And to help it pass I try to fabricate these stories
That aren't even mine, or anyone's, but see me through.
I'm in the country. I drive around all day, for the lack
Of anything to do, and for the beauty of the drive,
Along twisting country roads, a twitch away from death.
After dinner on the deck I congratulate myself
On where I am, while the evening deepens into dark
And fireflies appear. The sole reality is breath
Inflating the narrative of a life, wending its way
Across the decades page by repetitive page
Until it comes at last to nothing. There should be
More I guess, though I really don't believe it.
I love my moments in the sun as much as anyone,
And then I'm on my way, rowing gently down
The stream of consciousness like someone in a dream
Of a common language, adequate to its purposes
Or lack of them, until it suddenly hits a snag,
Or a random sentence breaks the spell:
James Wright: "I have wasted my life."
Rilke: "You must change your life."
But why? It feels convincing, but in the end
It's just more language, and it disappears.
Sometimes it touches on the truth, now and then
It sings, but for the most part it meanders on
Like a country road, leading not to some horror
But to the stupefying banality at the heart of things.

DOROTHY DEAN

I thought it was starting, and
In retrospect, I suppose it was. *Domes*
Won the Frank O'Hara Award (which killed it off),
And so to celebrate I bought a new green mackinaw
From L.L. Bean and headed for New York. I stayed at
John's, had lunch with an indifferent editor from Columbia U.P.
And hung around with friends. There was a party in a loft
Somewhere downtown—an exhibition of a hundred 2×2-inch
Paintings by George Schneeman, $25 each—and though I
Went there with a friend, I spent the whole night talking to a small
Black woman in a tailored dress who'd majored in philosophy at
   Harvard,
Where she'd studied Wittgenstein and Aristotle with my own
   advisor
Rogers Albritton—whom of course we talked about, along with
   Wittgenstein
And art and whether Wittgenstein was gay (such innocent days!).
She said there was a book that clinched the case, we swapped
   addresses
And I bought a painting and went back to John's, where Robert
   Dash
And Darragh Park, resplendent in tuxedos from the opera, were
   on display.
I passed around my tiny painting of some laundry on a clothesline.

"So he does have talent," John opined. It was an inauspicious
    meeting:
When we met again, Bob said that at the time they'd thought I
    was
(Despite that splendid mackinaw) another downtown bum.

Dorothy Dean turned out to be a minor figure in the Warhol
And *New Yorker* worlds. We carried on a desultory correspondence
For a few years, which included the book she claimed "spilled the
    gay beans
On Wittgenstein," but which it turned out I had read. Now and
    then
I'd come across her name: on Lou Reed's *Take No Prisoners,*
    where he
Channels Lenny Bruce ("We call her Tiny Malice, Dorothy
    Dean");
In a show of photographs of Max's Kansas City, where she'd bar
    the door;
As a footnote to my fascination with George Trow, who eulogized
    her
After she died of cancer in Colorado, where she'd moved in the
    eighties,
When she couldn't take New York anymore; in a poem of Robert
    Creeley's.
It didn't amount to anything, yet that's where time is measured—
At the intersections of your life with someone else's. Some of
    them

Are singular, some of them, like mine with Bob's and Darragh's,
    reoccur
Until somebody dies. You set out with a promise and a wish,
And live in them until the wish and its fulfillment start to seem
    routine
And the anecdotes begin, the moments that become life stories,
Like that evening over forty years ago I spent with Dorothy Dean.

I realize that almost everybody in this poem is dead now,
Tiny figures flickering through time. At a party at Poets House
Last May I saw a wonderful exhibition of some paintings
Of George Schneeman's of a bunch of poets with their clothes off.
Ron Padgett had co-organized the show, and he recalled that
Night of tiny paintings back in 1972. It was at Holly Solomon's loft,
He told me, and we talked about how they were made with Magic
    Markers,
Which couldn't take the sunlight. "If you bought one and just put
    it in a
Drawer it was OK," he said; "otherwise, in a few years it was gone."
That's what happened to mine: it went from Cambridge to
    Milwaukee,
Where my son was born, then to a house in Whitefish Bay, where
    I built a study
With a lot of bookshelves, propped it up and looked at it from time
    to time.
I want to resist the urge to sermonize: these connections never
    occurred to me

Until I started writing this, but that's how poetry carries you away.
I looked at it as long as I could see it, but it's gone now, like that
  house
And the backyard I could ponder from my study. I write in real
  time,
But the time I write about exists in my imagination, where I used
  to live
When I was starting out along the road to nowhere, following my
Reflection in the mirror of the future, watching my painting with
  its image
Of some laundry on a clothesline getting fainter and fainter each
  year;
And by the time Dorothy Dean died it had disappeared.

II

IDIOT WIND

Another idiot denounces American poets:
Give us more of the "we" we need, he demands,
And I agree, but so what? I do it constantly,
And I'm not alone. And yet we're so abstract,
So dispersed, so virtual I don't know who "we" are—
Not other poets certainly, or the people in the theaters
I frequent on weekends, watching movies of exploding trucks.
My mother weaned me on Emerson, though I didn't know it,
And Emerson (no idiot) railed against American poets too:
"Men of talents who sing, and not the children of music.
The argument is secondary, the finish of the verses primary."
I omitted an "is" in that quotation for the sake of finish,
And yet I think a poem *should* be the "metre-making argument"
Emerson called for, though the argument always peters out.
We try and try, and try and try again to get it right
Along the road to hell, but it never works: something
Off to one side derails it, or it loses focus, or the better angels
Of our nature wake, and then go back to sleep. Poems
Should be true, true to what we think—"to thine own self
Be true"—but then, what *do* we think? We reason in clichés—
Otherwise, we'd never move. Why should we deny
This truth about ourselves? Can't we see what we are?

TULSA

Always treat humanity, whether in yourself or in another person,
as an end in itself, and never simply as a means. **KANT**

It wasn't just the slaughter—though proportionally it
Exceeded all our other wars combined—but what prefigured it
And what it brought about. There was the cotton gin
That gave the South a one-commodity economy
It needed slaves to run. And slavery required power,
Political power, to perpetuate itself, and power depended on
New slave states to sustain it, so that when its grandiose fantasy
Of Manifest Destiny—a Caribbean empire absorbing Mexico and
    Cuba—
Collapsed by 1861, there wasn't anything left to do but secede.
It's sickening to read the rationales, because they cut so close.
    Mississippi:
"Our position is thoroughly identified with the institution of
    slavery—
The greatest material interest of the world. Its labor supplies the
    product
Which constitutes by far the largest and most important portions
Of commerce of the earth. These products are peculiar to the
    climate
Verging on the tropical regions, and by an imperious law of nature,
None but the black race can bear exposure to the tropical sun.

These products have become necessities of the world,
And a blow at slavery is a blow at commerce and civilization."
Georgia: "Because by their declared principles and policy
They have outlawed $3,000,000,000 of our property." Texas:
"That in this free government *all white men are and of right*
Ought to be entitled to equal civil and political rights;
That the servitude of the African race, as existing in these States,
Is mutually beneficial to both bond and free, and is abundantly
    authorized
And justified by the experience of mankind, and the revealed
Will of the Almighty Creator, as recognized by all Christian
    nations."

After a desultory start the carnage began in earnest, with standing
    charges—
The strategy Napoléon had used—into the teeth of modern
    ordnance
Scattering brains and blood and shattered bones across the open
    fields,
Until supplanted by the trenches that looked out upon the graves
    of WWI.
Sometimes the history of a war obscures the meaning of the war:
Behind the strategies and battles—Antietam and Gettysburg of
    course,
But also those whose names have vanished into books or onto
    Wikipedia,
Like Peebles' Farm or Philippi or Darbytown or Hoover's Gap—

The unconcluded narrative continued to unfold, conceived
In an original sin no ordinary victory or surrender could erase.
So when that victory finally came and the South gave up,
It was outwardly abolished, and the economic order it sustained
Went with the wind; but the souls of those who wrote those
    rationales
Remained unvanquished. As the bickering began, fatigue set in
And Reconstruction foundered. The Redeemers persevered,
The White League and the Red Shirts' organized campaigns of
    terror
Culminated in the Mississippi Plan of 1875, when the besieged
Republican electorate was shot or forced to flee, and Grant,
Fretting about Ohio, declined to intervene. The plan became a
    model
For the other states—South Carolina signed on too—until
    rendered obsolete
By the Compromise of 1877—the "Corrupt Bargain"—when in
    return
For the presidency, Rutherford B. Hayes agreed to pull all federal
    troops
From the South, which became, in effect, a separate nation after
    all.

That's the history part. I guess it's cynical and open to dispute:
There's the legend of the Lost Cause, that romanticized the way
    of life

The war destroyed, and Whiggish history, in which whites
   somehow forgot
"That blacks were creating thriving middle classes in many states
   of the South."
In 1999 I flew to Tulsa for a literary festival. There was the small
   city's
Usual downtown whose best days were behind it, and Oral Roberts
   University's
Enormous praying hands that pointed straight at heaven. The
   people
Who'd invited me showed me the sights (including those gigantic
   hands),
And during lunch one day described the riots that occurred in
   1921.
There was a vibrant black community in a part of town called
   Greenwood
(One of those thriving middle classes, I suppose), so prosperous
   with its
Banks and businesses and homes that it was called "the Negro
   Wall Street."
On Memorial Day there was an incident in an elevator in a
   downtown building
That involved a young white woman and a young black man, who
   was jailed
On suspicion of assault. A white crowd gathered, incited by an
   editorial

In the *Tulsa Tribune* egging on a lynching. Skirmishes ensued,
And then at last a huge white mob stormed into Greenwood, shooting
Indiscriminately, burning stores and businesses and houses, while biplanes
From an airfield near town, left over from WWI, dropped firebombs
And fired at people on the ground, until the Negro Wall Street lay in ruins.
No one really knows how many died—hundreds probably, and thousands wounded.
There's a modest monument today where Greenwood used to be,
But for over half a century the Tulsa Race Riot simply disappeared from history:
The copies of the *Tribune* with the editorial are missing from its archives
And the archives in the capitol; the riot itself went missing from the school
And history books, not just in Oklahoma and the South, but everywhere;
And there were never reparations. What flabbergasted me, beyond the riot itself,
Was the fact of its effacement, and the underlying explanation.
Dick Rowland—that was the young man's name—was just a stand-in
For the real cause: the black community's continually accumulating wealth,

That made its partial ownership of the oil companies that
   composed
The city's soul almost inevitable, but which was unacceptable.
   And so the
Pent-up anger was unleashed, and the worst episode of racial
Violence in the country's history vanished completely from its past.

In metaphysics and philosophy of language there's a view that
   holds
That if you want to know what something is, ignore what people
   say about it —
Look instead at where it came from. So much of what has plagued
   our
Politics for centuries now — the distrust of reason and the common
   good, of the ideal
Of justice; the obsession with the perfidy of government, a base
   conception of the social order —
Descended from the original sin of slavery and the desperate
   struggle to maintain it,
Before taking on a life of its own. "There goes the South for a
   generation,"
Johnson said as he signed the Civil Rights Act, though that was
   optimistic. The rhetoric
Of freedom floats upon the surface of a dark, unspoken dream of
   restoration,
Of a way of life that never actually existed, nurtured by a long
   forgetting.

The auction blocks and firebombs are gone, yet a straight line runs
    from
Charleston through Tulsa to today, and though the terms have
    changed,
The colors too—red and blue instead of black and white—the
    same resentments
And divisions linger, only now without the purpose that sustained
    them—
As though a nation had retained its sense of grievance, but lost its
    cause.
Sometimes I think I brood too much on these divides, but then I
    listen to the radio
Or watch TV and feel the hopelessness return. It's strange how
    anything as abstract
As the failure of some quaint ideal of human reciprocity, of the
    recognition
Of ourselves in others, could reverberate so long, and yet it has. I
    used to
Think philosophy and history didn't matter in the greater scheme
    of things:
That they were too remote from people's lives to make a difference,
As though the past were just another idle argument we kept
    repeating,
Without remembering what made it what it is. What it is
Is all around us, however difficult to see. And so the war goes on
In forms we can't quite recognize—accommodating children
Of an old obscenity still living in its lengthening shadow, in its
    shade.

IN THE LOUVRE

How many Crucifixions and bambini do I have to see
To realize these illustrations of the religion I was raised in
Aren't remotely true, as untrue as all those icons of mythology,
The statues in the basement—Venus with her missing arms,
Some satyrs, even Seneca, a man without transcendent qualities,
Gaunt and doomed as Jesus? How many pictures do I have to
    study
With a feigned enthusiasm till the whole thing feels like a scam
Facilitated by the greatest painters painting has ever known?
How many hordes of people studying them with comprehension
And sympathy do I have to look at till they start to seem like
    pagans
"Suckled in a creed outworn"?
                                 And yet I love the painting of St. Anne
With Mary and her baby on her lap. Freud argued that that smile,
Like Mona Lisa's in the gallery across the hall, was Leonardo's
    mother's,
Which you can make of what you choose, depending on your
    view of Freud.
Myths come and go and from a distance feel the same—strange
    icons
Of a "madness to explain" an unfamiliar world that passeth
    understanding
And never ends. From faith to superstition to regret: what started

As a screed becomes an elegy for a life deprived of illusions, a
    lament
For a certainty I thought I had but probably never did, of
    something
Beyond mere being. Why did I believe it, if I ever did?

CHAPPAQUIDDICK

I hate believing I grew up in a country
Better than the one I live in now. We were vaguely
Middle class: my mother was a schoolteacher,
My father a Navy NCO, a former concert violinist

Who cracked up—a "nervous breakdown"
As they called it then—when I was in the eleventh grade.
Sputnik woke the nation up, money poured in,
The San Diego schools were great, I played the clarinet,

Ran track, won science fairs and then went off to college
In the East, which I imagined would be paradise,
And indeed it was: the country turned out to be green
Instead of brown and tan, New York was new,

The rich were interesting and smart instead of just obscene,
And some of that enchantment trickled down to me.
It didn't last. There was Vietnam of course, but even then
There seemed to be a way to get it right: decency

And common sense, the individual life fulfilled
Within the confines of a common good.
People could create themselves, then finally retire,
The air felt full of possibilities deferred

But realized eventually, the national narrative
Was still in progress, one in which each person's life
Pursued a course that led from infancy to age.
It doesn't really matter whether all of this was true —

It seemed to be, then that perception changed.
When did the page turn and the past turn into paradise?
I remember watching TV shows about the future as a miracle,
With supersonic trains and flying cars and towers

Climbing to the sky. It's a disaster movie now,
A Depression-era song about ambition realized, and gone:
"I built a tower to the sun." I remember those towers
To the sun, and the trains that raced against time.

■

I travel a lot, I age, my mood and outlook change.
This week I came to see my granddaughter in Nashville
For the second time, big eyes and bald and smiling
In her Exersaucer with bright blocks and rings and a plastic fish.

On Saturday we went to Carnton Plantation, the site
Of the Battle of Franklin, the bloodiest encounter of the Civil
    War:
Two thousand dead in five hours, with the house turned into a
    hospital
And thirty or forty to a room, and stacks of amputated limbs.

Initially the dead were buried in an open field of shallow graves,
Their arms and legs protruding from the ground. Eventually
The village built a proper cemetery, with cypress trees protecting
Rows of regular stone blocks and Baby Lauren in her stroller.

In retrospect the battle was gratuitous: the war was lost,
The military part at least. Nashville is a new Milwaukee, cities
Situated at a confluence of the nation's economic winds:
Prosperity that flowed from immigration and industry and beer,

Followed by cheap labor and the drift of capital from there to
    here.
That's what the war was actually about: slavery was its cause,
But slavery was unsustainable—it was simply too egregious to
    endure.
It wasn't race that mattered, it was human property, and property
    is colorless,

Labor fungible—it's not important how it looks or sounds,
As long as it produces and shuts up: skyscrapers going up,
    restaurants,
Walmarts, football stadiums, neighborhoods that used to be slums
Suddenly sprouting boutiques, people anxiously content, and no
    real future.

I imagine the worst, because the truth is difficult to see.
Lauren, John and Annie, people like me are all going to be fine

(Though I'll be dead). But who'll keep it all? To ask that question
Is to answer it: as we drove past the new Nissan headquarters,

Silver in the sun, I thought about Milwaukee and Detroit
And how they're nobody's fault, because the question reaches back
To the poem of the past, and the dying fall of one last ode
To the Confederate dead, resting in victory beneath the cypress
    trees.

■

Sometimes there isn't any explanation for what happened,
Or the explanation is unsatisfying, since it rules out the possibility
Of a different outcome, of things turning out other than they did.
That's when the mind turns to fantasies and paranoia: we *want*
    them

To be different, as of course they would be but for—for *what*?
The assassinations? Altamont? For Charles Manson? Last month
Diane and I were on Martha's Vineyard, ground zero for the
    benign rich
I used to love, and in a way still do: there used to be a balance

Between civilization and its discontents, but then that balance
Altered, or continued only intermittently, in small pockets
Of privilege where wealth assumes a human scale. I read my
    poems,
We ate lobster rolls and drove around the island where they
    filmed *Jaws*,

Past Inkwell Beach, through Oak Bluffs and the Gothic cottages
Where Methodists once waited on the ending of the world, which
    didn't end.
The world never ends—what ends are explanations of the way
    it is.
I didn't know where Chappaquiddick was—a part of Martha's
    Vineyard

It turned out. I remember 1969, and how America was poised
    between
A recent past already turning into history, and a future that, in
    theory anyway,
Remained open. Nixon had finally got elected, but it didn't have
    to last—
We could still get back to where things started to collapse, and
    make it work.

I didn't care what shape it took, as long as it resumed the right
    direction.
I barely read the story in the *Times*, for there were other
    possibilities,
But one by one they fell away and 1972 became a debacle. True,
    there was
Watergate, but that was a holding action, as the country changed
    in ways

I could hardly see. I remember reading V. in college, a novel
About a search for something to explain a century, or simply
    someone's life.

Explanations like that don't exist: we harbor them because they're
    easy,
And because reality is numb. We took the ferry across a channel

Narrow enough to swim, we walked along a beach that dropped off
Steeply into Nantucket Sound. It was all gone: the party and its
    aftermath,
The lighted houses they passed on the way to the bridge,
The Oldsmobile that skidded off Dike Road and into Poucha
    Pond.

III

E.H.

Sometimes I stand in the middle of the floor,
Not going left, not going right. **STEPHEN SONDHEIM**

I like to get drunk and I like to write.
I search for ways in and can't find them,
But that doesn't mean they're not there. What isn't
There is the life between the words, the life that existed
Beyond the words, the life I don't have anymore.
In Michigan the feelings soaked the page,
Yet now they seem diminished in the telling
And no longer in our time, no longer of our place,
But in another country, one of an imagination
Anchored in a style; no longer in the stream
Or swamp, where the fishing was tragic.

I (whichever I this is) saw *Follies* last year.
The Weismann Girls come back to stand for what they were
And aren't anymore, in a theater slated for demolition.
Sally is a prisoner of her rage and imagination,
Pining for the magic of what might have been
Until the spell breaks, leaving her alone onstage
Amid the shards of her illusions. As she looks around
For what she is, all she can find is her age:
"I'm forty-nine. That's all I am."

Why do I get so angry? Why do I assume
The characters I love, the characters I love and hate?
There's a corruption from which I've never recovered
That diminishes me each day, until I can't tell which I am
Anymore, the mask or the face. The boat in Havana:
Last time was the last time. The stirring begins each night
And continues through the day here in a home that isn't home,
With Michigan far away, the finca far away, alone
In the vestibule in the early morning light, imagining
The feeling of cool steel against my forehead
And the sound of two drawers slamming.
I'm sixty-two. That's all I am.

AGAINST IMMORTALITY

Yes, the late night jazz, great sex and all
The human shit defining what we are:
Par for the course. I dwell instead
On minutiae, on little highs defining days
In need of definition: the package on the porch,
The email, the unexpected phone call.
These trivialities provide direction
And a sense of purpose to the small world
Each of us inhabits for a while
Until its time is finished, and it ends.
I know it feels like something to regret,
Yet why would anybody *want* to be immortal?
Immortality isn't what it used to be: the literary version
Comes too late to do you any good, and as for the immortal
Soul, what would it be *like* to lie awake for all eternity,
Without anything ever changing? Give me a break,
It seems to say: return me to the small world I remember,
Where there were surprises and disappointments
And I'd wake up each morning wondering what to do,
And to the fear of death. It energizes everything,
This terrible feeling of being just about to fall,
This terrifying feeling of contingency. Instead it
Offers you the life I'm desperate to escape:
The relief from care, from wanting life to change
For better or for worse; the sitting still.
    Shantih   shantih   shantih.
No packages, no emails, no phone calls.

EARLY APRIL IN THE COUNTRY

I'm here at my house, sitting on the deck
And looking at a landscape from which the snow has
Mostly disappeared, though the trees remain bare.
On the apple tree there's that fucking cardinal
Who reappears each year, plotting to shit on my car
Before I leave in the morning. The sun feels weak
Setting behind the trees, the light seems watery and vague
And on the hill that rises beyond Haney Ridge Road
At the bottom of the meadow I can see a scattering of
Indifferent cows arranged to form a static, pastoral tableau.
". . . the copper-, cream-, and chocolate-colored /
Cows we bought in Salzburg form a tiny herd." I remember
Writing those lines in my first "grand" poem, "Domes,"
Which I worked on for over a month in nineteen sixty-nine.
"We Poets in our youth begin in gladness," and while it didn't
Feel too much like gladness at the time, it saw me through,
Whatever it was, until now I feel this precarious combination
Of futility and pride that something real got completed
That left everything unchanged. The promise hangs in the air
As long as it can, and though eventually it starts to fade,
Its question mark survives, and remains unanswered.
"To strive, to seek, to find"—that was my favorite poem in
High school, before I knew anything, before I'd written anything,
Before anything had *happened*. I've shored it against the day

When consciousness flickers out and everything goes on:
Cows on the hillside. Cardinal in the apple tree. The world
Doesn't end with someone's awareness of it—it persists
Whether anyone considers it or not, leaving me alone
And wanting more, with that original ambition becoming
Fainter and fainter, reduced to reading and rereading
My old and not-so-old, my grand and not-so-grand poems.
They flowed, they had too many words, they were
Driven by a "madness to explain" that feels quaint now,
As though there were nothing to explain anymore.

FEAR AND TREMBLING

I had to read it the summer before I left for college.
I had a job running a miniature merry-go-round
With dinky airplanes instead of horses, across the street
From the zoo and the natural history museum,
Where I'd read a book that eventually changed my life,
Although I didn't realize it then. It was all about
Not being sure and being sure. It was about the sun of faith
Obscured by the cloud of not knowing. It was about being great.
And after fifty years I'm reading it again, and after fifty years
I'm back in San Diego for my high school class's fiftieth reunion,
Herbert Hoover High School '63. If you had told me then
What I'd be doing now or who I'd be I wouldn't have believed
     you—
Time is unimaginable until it passes, like the individual life
With which it coincides. And as for God, I didn't believe it then,
And yet it still made sense to me, and doesn't now. It was a
     metaphor
For being free, since listening to God meant listening to yourself.
A life is made up out of everything it can and can't imagine,
Had and didn't want, wanted and couldn't have—all of it there
In the yearbook for God to see. I wear a name tag with my
Picture circa 1963, carry a drink and wander around the lobby
Of the Lafayette Hotel, glancing down to place each face
Before moving on to the next one, staring into a hotel mirror
At the image of that distant boy who turned out to be me.

Maybe I make too much of things. Kierkegaard did,
Hung up in a no-man's-land between sacrifice and murder,
Between morality and mystery, conjuring up possibilities
Where there were none to see. My Moriah is a fantasy
Of living in the present, of inhabiting the interval
Between the settled past and the illusion of the future,
Which keeps receding. The tale may be superstitious bullshit,
Yet what resonates is the absence of anxiety, the sense
Of purpose, the uncertainty. Greatness is the underlying theme,
But it's invisible: greatness is the absolute, and it remains
    unknown.
I know the story that came true is not the one I set about to write,
Though it's the one I meant, the one I learned in high school.
Standing around a swimming pool, listening to pre-Beatles rock
    and roll,
Then flying back across the continent to tell my tale to anyone
Who'll listen: it's complete except for the conclusion,
Which remains unwritten, since it's inconceivable. What's left
Is wonder, wonder and waiting, canvassing the possibilities:
Respite or catastrophe, anonymity or validation—the abrupt
    angel,
The finality, the stayed hand; the ram caught in the shrubbery.

THE TENDERNESS OF MATHEMATICS

God created the integers, all else is the work of man.

LEOPOLD KRONECKER

He didn't do even that, since he doesn't exist,
And yet they're there: 0, 1, 2, 3 dot dot dot
Ad infinitum. And if Frege was right
(And certainly he was), they descended from
The basic principles of thought, from what we know
If we know anything at all. And yet they constantly surprise:
From out of nowhere number theory gets reflected
In the properties of automorphic forms, the distribution
Of the primes seems like the distribution of the stars
In their indifference to us, and the Eightfold Way,
That leads from Plato's paradise to here, starts out as idle
Speculation, combing through some symmetry groups,
Until the quarks pop out and bathe us in the world.

How can something so abstruse and abstract feel so close
And be so far away? "They force themselves upon us,"
Gödel remarked of the axioms of set theory, and he was right:
*Like some watcher of the skies / When a new planet
Swims into his ken*, we seem to see the units rearranged
Before our eyes, as what had been implicit all along
Suddenly seems clear. It doesn't happen in life, in real life,

Yet mathematics is a part of life. In high school
I thought I'd proved a theorem about perfect numbers.
The proof contained a fallacy, but for a week or so
I felt like stout Cortez upon his peak in Darien.
The dream of mathematics is of an underlying order
We invented without knowing it, waiting there
Just out of reach, waiting to manifest itself
And for its truths to intrude upon a consciousness
Asleep in its dream, asleep in no one's dream.

LA DURÉE

Proust read Bergson, then he wrote his poem.
I thought if I read Bergson too I'd figure out a way
To say what I've been gesturing at all my life
Without success: *la durée*, duration, time,
My own time, by which I mean your own time too.
I don't know why: the days go by without event,
Resembling one another in the main and in the details,
Each remaining individual in its moment as it
Disappears. The gray day dawns and turns to snow
Accumulating on the cars and on the parking lot
Below my window, other cars roll by along the street
I can see from my desk, while Henri Bergson floats adrift
On confusions about quantity and quality, and I—
I go on reading. Chapter Two: riffings about numbers
By a man who gave up mathematics for philosophy
Too soon, and missed what they'd discovered—
Numbers aren't constructed out of space or human time,
But from a pure idea of order at some Key West of the mind
Beyond duration and experience, where they last forever.
It's a great idea, yet we live in time, and here Bergson is right:
Each moment represents a whole—a whole of *what*? It's
There I start to lose him, as he wonders off into peculiar notions
Of succession, space and time—I want to throw his book against
    the
Wall as Wittgenstein did whenever he read Hume. The whole

Has got to be a life, an ordinary, individual life, a singular
Existence rounded with a sleep, contained in its entirety in every
Moment, like a pageant bathing in the light of an eternal now.
Sometimes I don't believe a word I say, and then remember why:
I think that everyone's as vexed by time as I am, and because I do
I grab whatever rhetoric comes my way. Of course there's
Something to be said for reticence and tact, but also something to be
Said for passionate abstraction, and for letting contradictions flow
Before relaxing back into reflection and the present tense
And nothing new to say. The poetry of life feels inexhaustible,
But it advances haltingly, besieged by second thoughts
And doubts—basking in the present, then returning to the past
For substance; wandering out into the open, then retreating
Back into the soul's small room; while all the while
Attempting to articulate a single thought constructed out of
Two opposing ones: that life is little; and that life is all.

I don't think this is Bergson: his duration isn't time at all,
At least not time as I conceive it—his duration is a tune
Played by sensations melting into one another to compose a life.
That's what perplexes me in Proust: that those involuntary
Memories awakened by a cookie or the paving stones of Venice
Coalesce into a swoon that lasts three thousand pages.
He thinks everything exists at once, and nothing vanishes
In the chaos of society and sex, or in the small delights
Of coffee and a newspaper; that time returns us to ourselves;
That time restores the flavor of those hours that flourished once
And still survive within the confines of a little phrase.

Bergson: "Pure duration is the form which the succession
Of our conscious states assumes when our ego lets itself *live.*"
I just don't get it: my experience of time is so confined,
So limited to *now.* Instead of ranging back and forth
Across successive years, I occupy the span of my attention,
Like a mirror that reflects itself and thus exhibits nothing.
This morning in the *Times* there was a piece about an exhibition
At the Morgan on *Swann's Way.* It quoted from an elegant
Notebook Jacques Bizet's mother gave to Proust: "Should it be a
    novel,
A philosophical essay, am I a novelist?" Is this a poem, an essay,
Or another form of exercise in time, which after all is what poems
    are?
It's what I think, or want to say: time can't be pictured or described,
But what those accidental memories, so trivial and insignificant
In themselves, provide is the experience of pure duration, of an
    interval
Between what happened once and now that measures what we are
And makes us human—not a life recaptured, but a life defined.
Perhaps that *is* what Bergson meant to say, when you abstract away
From all the rhetoric and fallacies: that *la durée* is just the form
A life assumes in retrospect, or that emerges in the contours of a
    poem.
There's a Fitzgerald story, "The Curious Case of Benjamin
    Button,"
Whose ending always moves me. The protagonist is born old,
A seventy-year-old baby, and his life develops in reverse:

A successful hardware business, marriage and a child, the
    charge up
San Juan Hill, then Harvard football, prep school, an inexorably
Diminishing adolescence, immaturity and infancy, as he ages
    backwards
Into birth and nonexistence. It's narrated in Fitzgerald's
    characteristic
Clipped romantic style and made a so-so movie. What haunts me
Is the blankness at the end, the rounding sleep. Of course that
    sleep
Encompasses both ends, but since our own lives ramble on
From day to day and line to line, their end is open and uncertain
And their contours indistinct. But this one ambles backwards
Towards an end that always lies conspicuously in view,
So you can grasp it as a limited totality, and trace its shape.

All this is written from a single point of view, my own,
Since that's how time presents itself to me. But real time,
Objective time—the time of history, prehistory and cosmology—
Is something Bergson didn't understand, and I don't either,
Even though I live in it. "Lift your head, look out the window"—
Standard exhortations to forget about yourself and breathe,
And I agree with all of them, and still I don't know what to do.
Love, of course, and sex, but they confine you to yourself
In a kingdom of two, which is what I'm trying to transcend.
Physics helps: a vision of the world beyond appearance
As it is in itself and not from anyone's particular perspective,

Measured by the clocks of mathematics that preceded our
Existence and continue ticking after everyone has gone.
That vision may be one more insubstantial pageant,
Or simply too abstract and literal to actually believe. Maybe
The better way is simply to remain indifferent, but again,
It's one thing to propose it and another thing to see it through.
I remember one time when the feeling of my own existence
    faltered,
About a year after I'd settled in Milwaukee. I was in a Kmart
Parking lot—a local version of the paving stones of Venice—
And couldn't understand why I was there or what had brought me
    there.
I fell into a mild depression that persisted for a year or so
And dissipated, leaving me as I am, and as I've been for forty years.
There may be various ways to organize one's story, structuring it
By place-names or by people or by poems, instead of incidents
And years, yet all of them seem equal in the end. A life's
Partitions are internal to it, and of no significance beyond its
    course.
I can live with that: my own time represents the world to me,
Although I realize it isn't real time at all—and so what?
It keeps me going, incident by incident, chapter by chapter,
Waiting on a dénouement that keeps receding into the fog
Of the future, and meanwhile living in a present illuminated
By the glow of the past, and in its shade. This has been a
Poem about time, but see how much of it is visual and spatial,
Just as Bergson said. I didn't read the chapter on free will,
But I can guess at it: we have it, of course, thanks to an obscure

Philosophy. Sometimes a single idea is enough—*la durée*,
Whatever it might mean. I think I live it every day,
Waking every morning to the next episode of a narrative
Whose origin lies beyond the reach of memory, whose
Conclusion is unwritten and whose logic is the free
Association of sensations and desires, governed by appetites
Even in extremis—like Proust, at the end of his duration,
Sending out for a peach, an apricot and iced beer from the Ritz.
I'm hungry. I think I'll get a hamburger at Dr. Dawg.

COVERS BAND IN A SMALL BAR

They make it feel like yesterday,
Which is the whole idea: another dateless
Saturday in the basement of Charter Club,
Drinking beer and listening to a Trenton covers band
Play Four Tops songs: "Sugar Pie, Honey Bunch,"
"It's the Same Old Song." They occupied my mind
In 1966 through dinner with Robbie at Del Pezzo, later
In the Vassar Club and on a cruise around Manhattan
For Peter Mahony's parents' wedding anniversary.
My tastes "evolved": more Stax, less Motown,
Then the Velvet Underground and IQ rock—
God, I was a snob. And now Lou Reed is dead
And I'm sitting in the Art Bar in Milwaukee,
Long past my usual bedtime—*I don't stay out late,*
Don't care to go / I'm home about eight, just me
And my radio—listening to my favorite songs again,
Hearing them as though for the first time? Not at all:
They're too familiar, I'm too preoccupied with them,
Even though the flesh is still willing—swaying
Slightly at the table, nodding up and down
To the memory of "Sugar Pie, Honey Bunch,"
To the melody of "Pale Blue Eyes."

VICARIOUS MELANCHOLIA

It fills up the space where poems used to be,
Until there's no space left. It's incessant
Phone calls, figuring out money and flights to
Somewhere, nowhere, not knowing what comes next:
There's nowhere to go, which is the problem
(I think everything's the problem) taking its toll.
Diane looked at me cross-eyed at lunch and I sank
Into a depression I recalled from forty years ago:
The constant consciousness of helplessness;
The constant feeling of inevitability, of the anger
At that feeling; of the separateness of persons.
Talk is like drugs, repeating what I said each night
In the morning, and on the phone each afternoon:
A different hospital each time, then the same hospital.
A fear of selfishness, an imperative of self-defense:
These are the boundaries of my life now,
The borderlines of my existence for a while.

"In the midst of life we are in death." Any
Person's death diminishes me, and yet the fear of
Death is something one can only face alone.
Poetry is stylized indifference, a drawing back
From the divide between my life and its negation —
Not because it's empty, but because it's full, too full,

Full of someone else's. Coming home each day
To the message light blinking on the phone,
My heart sinks as I press the button, and the dial tone
Comes as a relief, since I don't know what to do.
It's easier in miniature, within the limits of the page,
The confines of a single consciousness, with the drama
All offstage until the phone rings and it starts again.

THE AGE OF ANXIETY

                                    isn't an historical age,
But an individual one, an age to be repeated
Constantly through history. It could be any age
When the self-absorbing practicalities of life
Are overwhelmed by a sense of its contingency,
A feeling that the solid body of this world
Might suddenly dissolve and leave the simple soul
That's not a soul detached from tense and circumstance,
From anything it might recognize as home.
I like to think that it's behind me now, that at my age
Life assumes a settled tone as it explains itself
To no one in particular, to everyone. I like to think
That of those "gifts reserved for age," the least
Is understanding and the last a premonition of the
Limits of the poem that's never done, the poem
Everyone writes in the end. I see myself on a stage,
Declaiming, as the golden hour wanes, my long apology
For all the wasted time I'm pleased to call my life —
A complacent, measured speech that suddenly turns
Fretful as the lights come up to show an empty theater
Where I stand halting and alone. I rehearse these things
Because I want to and I can. I know they're quaint,
And that they've all been heard before. I write them
Down against the day when the words in my mouth
Turn empty, and the trapdoor opens on the page.

A PRIVATE SINGULARITY

I used to like being young, and I still do,
Because I think I still am. There are physical
Objections to that thought, and yet what
Fascinates me now is how obsessed I was at thirty-five
With feeling older than I was: it seemed so smart
And worldly, so fastidiously knowing to dwell so much
On time—on what it gives, what it destroys, on how it feels.
And now it's here and doesn't feel like anything at all:
A little warm perhaps, a little cool, but mostly waiting on my
Life to fill it up, and meanwhile living in the light and listening
To the music floating through my living room each night.
It's something you recognize in retrospect, long after
Everything that used to fill those years has disappeared
And they've become regrets and images, leaving you alone
In a perpetual present, in a nondescript small room where it began.
You find it in yourself: the ways that led inexorably from
Home to here are simply stories now, leading nowhere anymore;
The wilderness they led through is the space behind a door
Through which a sentence flows, following a map in the heart.
Along the way the self that you were born as turns into
The person you created, but they come together at the end,
United in the memory where time began: the tinkling of a bell
On a garden gate in Combray, or the clang of a driven nail

In a Los Angeles backyard, or a pure, angelic clang in Nova
   Scotia—
Whatever age restores. It isn't the generalizations I loved
At thirty-five that move me now, but single moments
When my life comes into focus, and the feeling of the years
Between them comes alive. Time stops, and then resumes its story,
Like a train to Balbec or a steamer to Brazil. We moved to San
   Diego,
Then I headed east, then settled in the middle of the country
Where I've waited now for almost forty years, going through the
Motions of the moments as they pass from now to nothing,
Reading by their light. I don't know why I'm reading them again—
Elizabeth Bishop, Proust. The stories you remember feel like
   mirrors,
And rereading them like leafing through your life at a certain age,
As though the years were pages. I keep living in the light
Under the door, waiting on those vague sensations floating in
And out of consciousness like odors, like the smell of sperm and
   lilacs.
In the afternoon I bicycle to a park that overlooks Lake Michigan,
Linger on a bench and read *Contre Sainte-Beauve* and *Time
   Reborn*,
A physics book that argues time is real. And that's my life—
It isn't much, yet it hangs together: its obsessions dovetail,
As the private world of my experience takes its place
Within a natural order that absorbs it, but for a while lets it live.

It feels like such a miracle, this life: it promises everything,
And even keeps its promise when you've grown too old to care.
It seems unremarkable at first, and then as time goes by it
Starts to seem unreal, a figment of the years inside a universe
That flows around them and dissolves them in the end,
But meanwhile lets you linger in a universe of one:
A village on a summer afternoon, a garden after dark,
A small backyard beneath a boring California sky.
I said I still felt young, and so I am, yet what that means
Eludes me. Maybe it's the feeling of the presence
Of the past, or its disappearance, or both of them at once —
A long estrangement and a private singularity, intact
Within a tinkling bell, an iron nail, a pure, angelic clang —
The echo of a clear, metallic sound from childhood,
Where time began: "Oh, beautiful sound, strike again!"

THE PHYSICAL ETERNAL

Its beginning lasts forever, and it never fades.
In a universe that nothing made, to look outwards
In any direction is to look into a past so utterly
Remote and so difficult to see that it could only be
An afterimage of the mind, of what a mind conceived:
Some residual radiation waiting to be deciphered
By no one, or by us. What seems incredible
Is that anything so magnificent should remain
So meaningless, even with all the virtually inaudible
Human static blended in, since nothing is ever lost
And all the information is retrieved—which God alone
Can read, although there is no God. We only grasp
What's real by analogies—an individual history,
A history of the universe—that don't make any sense:
As a life is made up out of moments or a book
Is made of pages, so the whole is to its fragments,
Like the remnants of what must have happened
In a nanosecond nearly fourteen billion years ago
Or on an afternoon in 1983, still hanging there
In the background, hanging around forever.

THE SWIMMER

It was one of those midsummer Sundays . . .

JOHN CHEEVER

Photo: sitting by the cabin on Lake Au Train
We rented every summer, reading John Cheever,
Then rowing out in a boat after dinner to fish.
The light would turn golden, then start to fade
As I headed home, past a new log dream house
I could see from our porch, and wished I could own.
I was married then and lived in my imagination,
Writing the poems I was sure would make my name
Eventually, and meanwhile waiting out the afternoons
Within the limits of a world that never changed,

The world of stories. I was almost thirty-eight,
With the compulsion to immortalize myself
That comes with middle age and disappointment.
I knew what I imagined and desired, yet didn't know,
For even though desire can delineate the contours
Of a life, its true substance is beyond desire
And imagination, unrecognizable until it's happened.
In seven years the substance of my future changed:
Instead of summers on the lake, I found myself alone
And free, not wanting what I'd wanted anymore,

And happy. Happiness, unhappy people say,
Comes in degrees, and yet it isn't true. The same
Ambitions and desires, the same attachments
And designs can constitute two different worlds—
A world I'd lived in and a world I never knew
Until I entered it, and made it mine. I wrote a long,
Meandering poem on marriage and its aftermath
That argued (if a poem can argue) that it never ends,
But stays suspended in time, like an afternoon
In August in our small cabin, with the television on

And the lake still visible beyond the door.
It's all still there, in that decade out of mind
I never think about anymore, until some moment
In a movie, or in a story I thought I'd read
And hadn't, or read and can't remember
Brings it back, and then I'm thirty-eight again,
The future still uncertain and there for the taking,
Which is what I did, though I didn't know it—
Which doesn't matter now, for though those wishes
Did come true, it wasn't as I'd dreamed them.

"The Monkey's Paw" is a story about three wishes—
The first one a disaster, the second one an unintended
Horror it takes the last wish to dissolve—that ends
On an empty street. My story is not so dramatic,
Yet the ending feels the same: I have the life

I wanted, people know my name, music fills the rooms
Each evening and each day renews the miracle,
And yet it's not the same. The real world can never
Realize a fantasy lived in the imagination,
That only felt like heaven while it wasn't there.

I thought I'd read "The Swimmer" sitting by the lake
Those thirty-something years ago, but when I looked at it
Last week I couldn't remember reading it at all. It's a story
Devastating on its face—an allegory of the dissolution
Of its hero, who on a beautiful suburban afternoon
Sets out for home by way of swimming pools and alcohol.
His quest begins in confidence and gladness, but as its course
Unfolds its tenor starts to change, as the watercolor
Light begins to fade, the air turns colder and he ages visibly,
Until it ends in autumn, darkness and an empty house.

The moral of the allegory is implicit, but it seems to me
More moving read another way—as a reimagining
Of a life from the perspective of disillusionment and age.
It still starts on a summer afternoon, but a remembered one.
Instead of youth and confidence and hope dissolving,
They're already gone, and instead of a deteriorating world,
It's an indifferent one. I feel at home in this amended parable:
It fits the way a story ought to fit, and it even feels true.
Sitting in my house in the country, there isn't much to do
But stare at the trees through the patio doors open to the deck.

It's not the dream house I remember, but at least it's mine,
And at least I'm happy, though I've lately come to recognize
That happiness is not what it's cracked up to be. As for poetry,
Poetry turned out fine, though nobody actually cares about it
In the old sense anymore. That's the trouble with stories —
They need to come to a conclusion and to have a point,
Whereas the point of growing old is that it doesn't have one:
Someone sets out on an afternoon, following his predetermined
Course as all around him summer darkens and the leaves turn
    sere,
And finally arrives at home, and finds there's nothing there.

ACKNOWLEDGMENTS

Some of the poems in this book have been published (some in slightly different form) in the following magazines:

The American Scholar: "The Arrogance of Physics," "Dorothy
    Dean," "The Tenderness of Mathematics"
Aphros: "Against Immortality"
Boston Review: "Von Freeman"
Classic Toy Trains: "Frank Sinatra's Trains"
Copper Nickel: "Idiot Wind"
Hanging Loose: "A Coupla Yeggs"
Kenyon Review: "*La Durée*"
The New Republic: "Skinny Poem"
The New Yorker: "Covers Band in a Small Bar"
The Ocean State Review: "The Long Dissolve"
The Paris Review: "The Swimmer"
Poetry: "A Private Singularity"
Poetry Northwest: "The Japanese Aesthetic"
Prelude: "Chappaquiddick"
Raritan: "The Age of Anxiety," "In the Louvre"
The Saint Ann's Review: "Early April in the Country"
Smartish Pace: "Melancholy of the Autumn Garden," "Sartor
    Resartus"
Southwest Review: "Little Guys Who Live Here"
Tin House: "Miss Heaton," "The Physical Eternal"
The Yale Review: "*Fear and Trembling*"

"Tulsa" was commissioned by the Smithsonian Institution and published in a volume of poems and photographs, *Lines in Long Array*, commemorating the sesquicentennial of the Civil War.

"E.H." and "Vicarious Melancholia" were published in Poem-a-Day, an online feature of the Academy of American Poets.

"The Uninvolved Narrator" appeared in a chapbook published by the magazine *Coldfront*.

"Frank Sinatra's Trains" was published as a broadside by Woodland Pattern Book Center in Milwaukee.

"A Private Singularity" was republished on the website Poetry Daily.